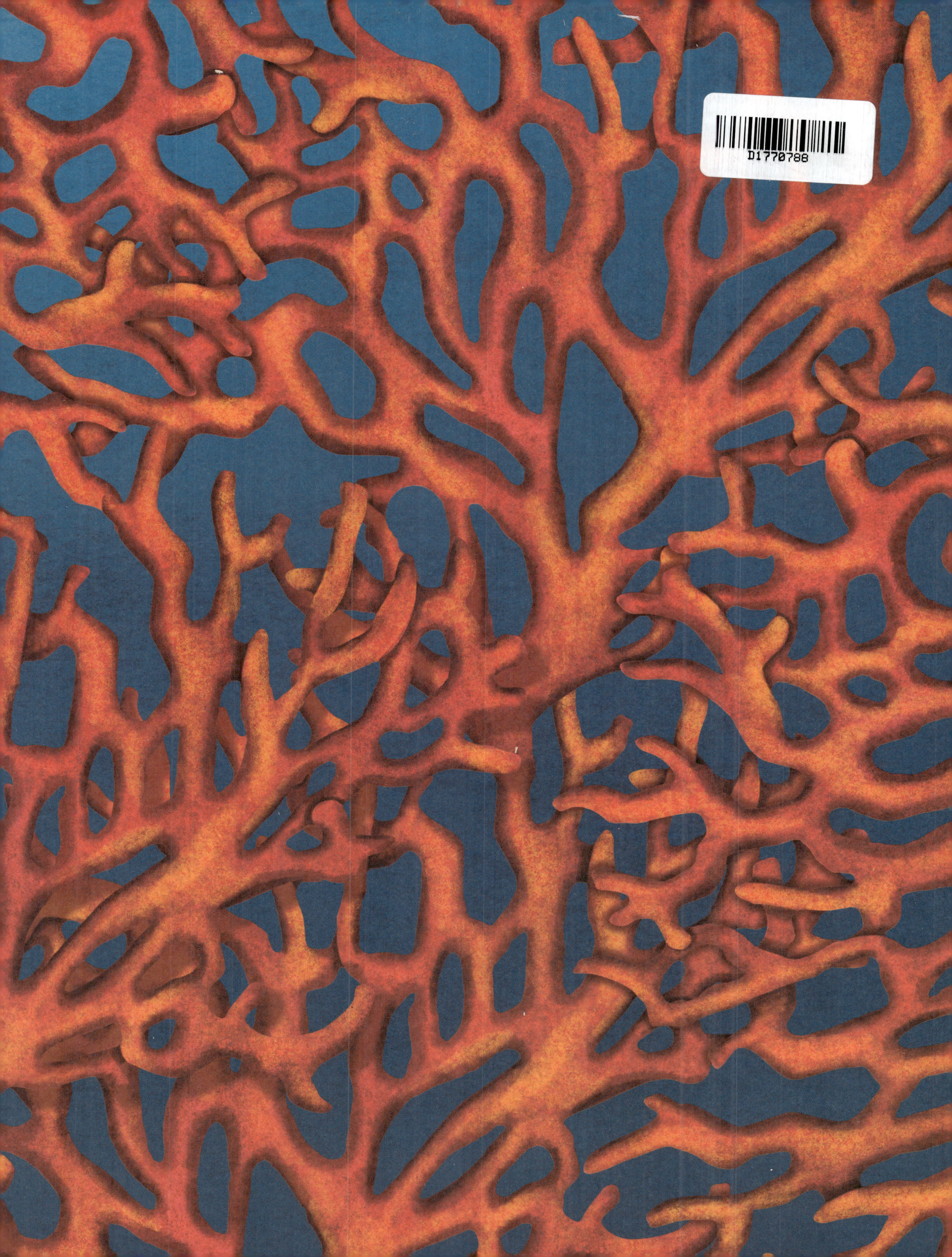

vmb
PUBLISHERS

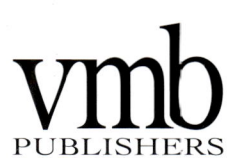

The Big Book of Giant Sea Creatures

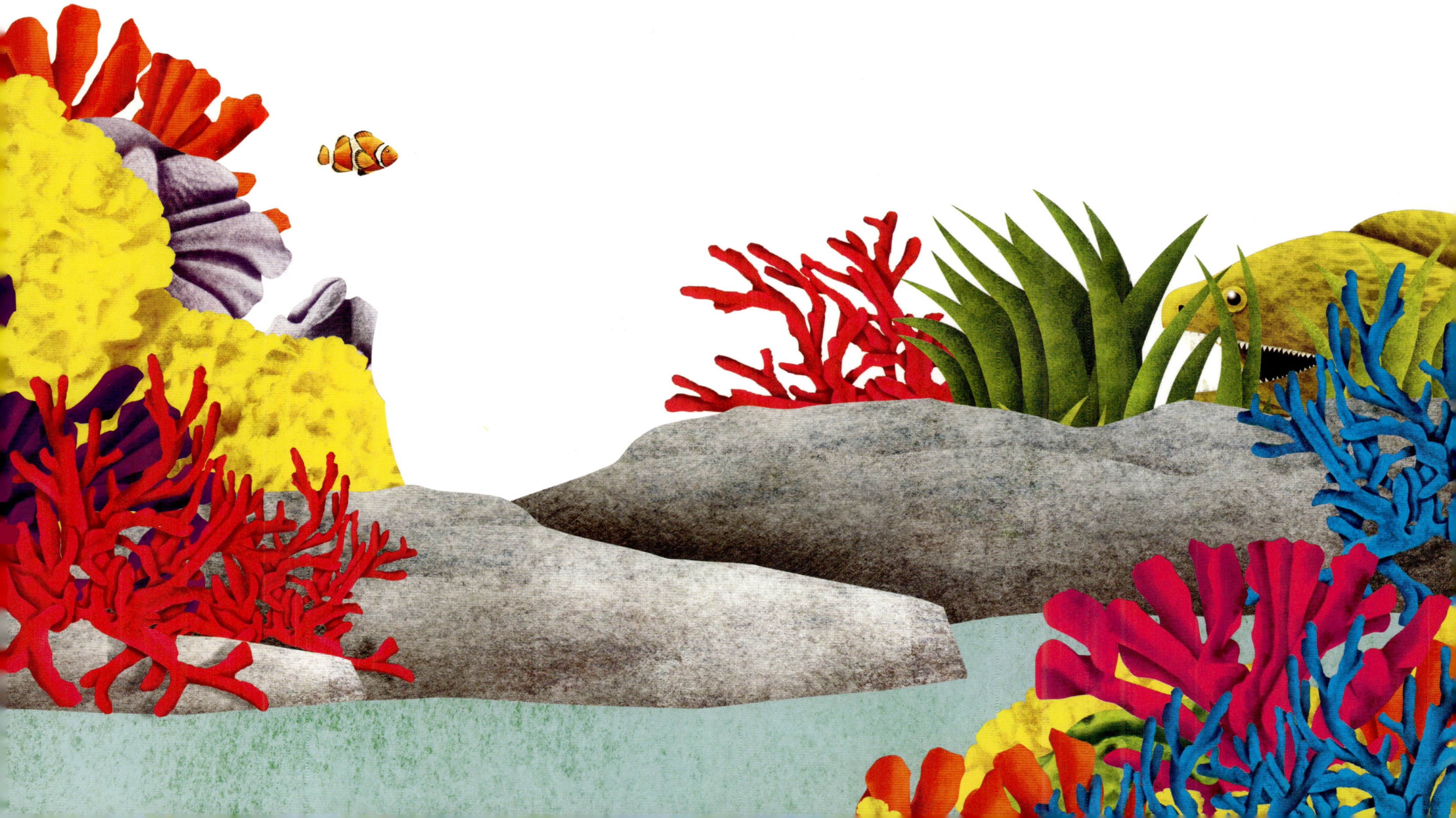

Introduction

Perhaps you already know that marine waters cover more than **70% of the surface of the Earth**, and that in some places the ocean is deeper than Mount Everest is tall. All this space is available for **millions of animal species**, including fish, mollusks, dolphins, whales, crustaceans, jellyfish, starfish, and many more. The sea is home to some of **our planet's largest inhabitants**, like the huge blue whale and the peaceable whale shark. The oceans can support and feed lots of giant creatures because there is plenty of food for them all.

But that's not all: the buoyancy of water can also support their enormous weight. There are animals that prefer to live in the open sea and others in the warm waters of the coral reef, while there are those that pass their lives in the abyssal zone.
However, the lives of all these creatures are full of surprises that will amaze and excite you as you enter this fantastic world that, to a great extent, is still mysterious.

Lion's Mane Jellyfish

This solitary jellyfish lives in the cold waters of the Pacific Ocean and can be found as far as the Arctic, allowing itself to be **carried by the ocean's currents**. Its curious name derives from the yellow-red color of the **numerous** hair-like **tentacles** hanging from the underside of its body, surrounding the mouth. The tentacles, which are over 98 feet (30 m) long, are covered in **stinging cells** that release a paralyzing toxin upon contact. The lion's mane jellyfish can also produce **its own light**, which glows dimly in the dark depths of the ocean.

Its head is 6.5 feet (2 m) wide. It feeds on fish and crustaceans.

They form large swarms when there are storms.

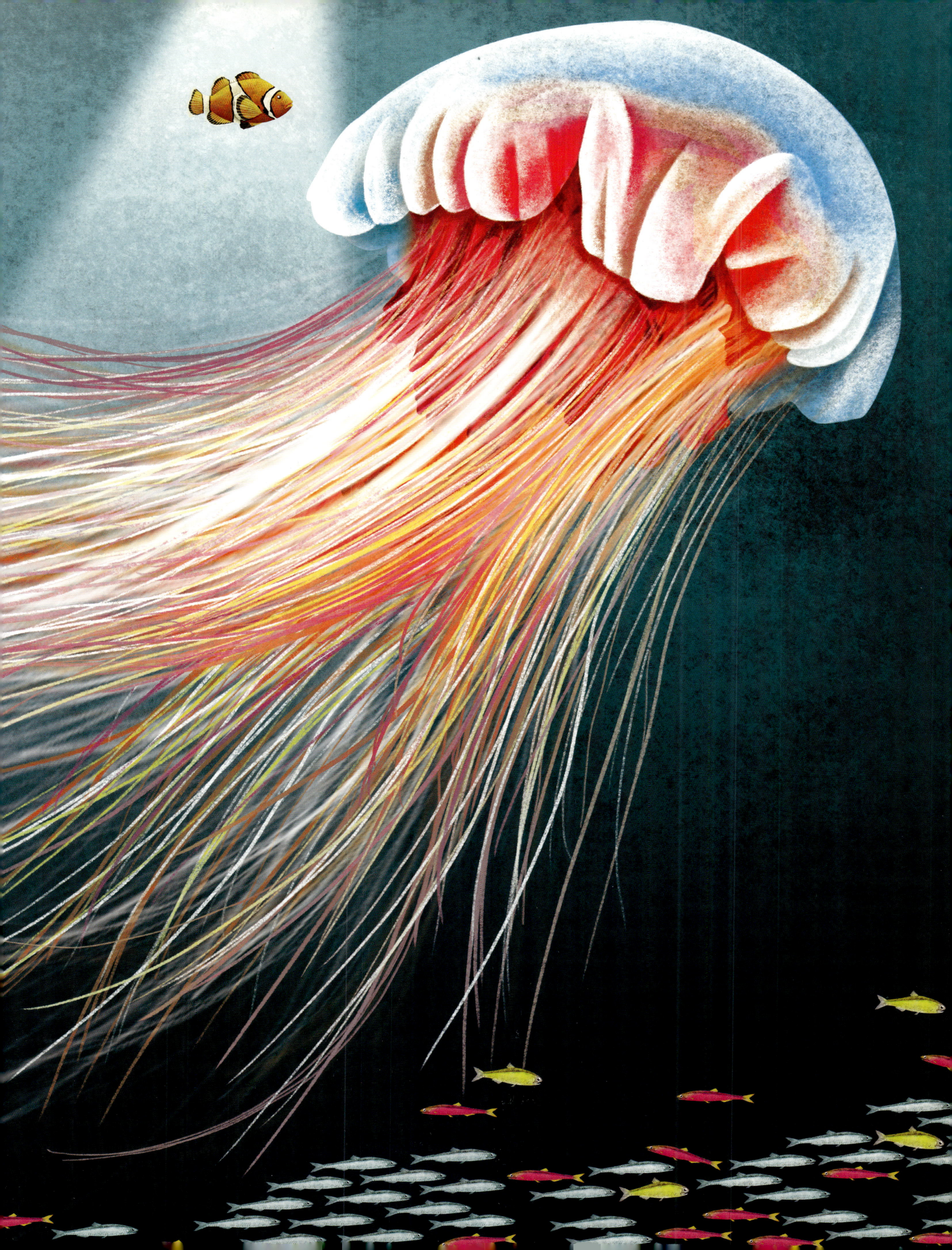

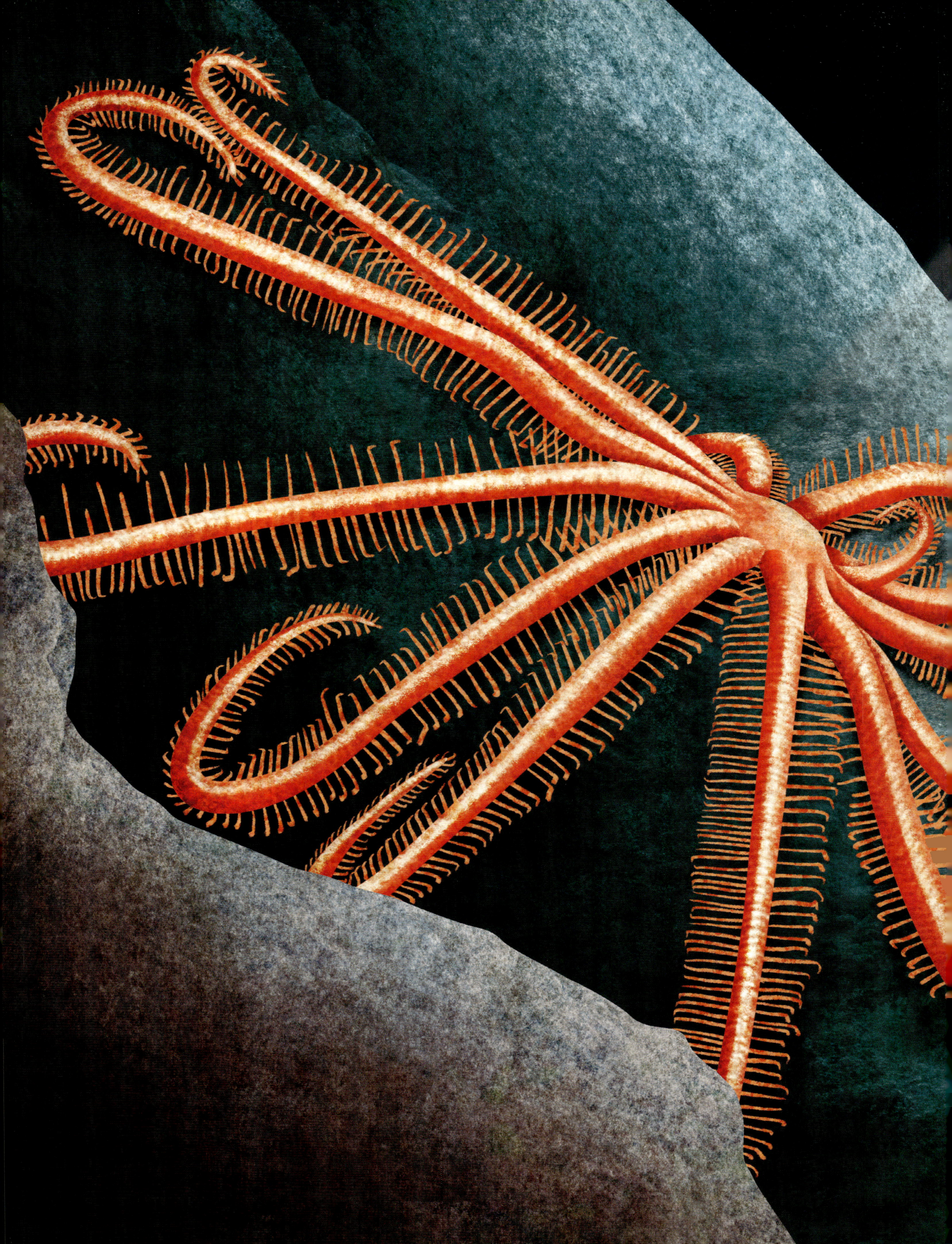

Giant Sea Star

It is very **rare** to come across this huge starfish because it lives in extremely deep waters in the Gulf of Mexico. It is **bright red** and, despite its size, looks very delicate. It can grow up to 12 arms, which are **very long and thin**. They are attached to a **circular body** that has a maximum diameter of just 1 inch (2.5 cm). Unlike other starfish, which are ferocious predators, the giant sea star feeds itself by simply raising some of its many arms, which are covered with **fine structures** similar to stiff hairs, to trap tiny particles carried by ocean currents.

Including its thin arms, it has a diameter of 4.6 feet (1.4 m). It feeds on plankton, which it collects by filtering the water.

Blue Whale

This gigantic queen of the oceans generally **migrates over long distances**: in summer it heads towards **colder polar waters** where there are plenty of **krill** to eat, which the whale filters from the water with its **baleen**. It spends the rest of the year in the warmer waters of the **tropics**, where the females give birth to their calves. The blue whale can stay submerged for up to **20 minutes** before having to resurface for air. It has an excellent **system for communicating**: it emits **sounds** that can be heard by its fellow creatures **thousands of miles away**, in the depths of the ocean.

Measuring 110 feet (33.5 m), it is the largest animal to have ever existed on Earth.

Its pectoral fins can reach a length of 10–13 feet (3–4 m)!

Great White Shark
It can be as long as 21 to 23 feet (6.5–7 m) and can swim at speeds of over 37 mph (60 km/h).

The great white shark is considered one of the most **ferocious ocean predators**. It has 3-inch (7.5-cm) **pointed teeth** that are razor-sharp, and rows of **replacement teeth** should they fall out. Very few animals are safe from its jaws. As well as fish, its favorite prey are seals and penguins, but it can also overpower **whales and dolphins**. It likes to live in both cold and warm waters, where its potential prey are abundant. It has an **excellent sense of smell** and can detect blood up to **3 miles (5 km)** away. **The pups** are already 5 feet (1.5 m) long when they are born, and they are **not looked after by their mother**, who may even **eat them**.

The manta ray is a very big, flat fish. Its **pectoral fins** are so well-developed **they look like wings**, and indeed this animal swims **so gracefully and rhythmically** that it looks like a bird in flight. "Manta" is a Spanish word that means **cape**, which refers to its large fins. Like whales, it feeds on plankton, which it collects by channeling water into its gaping mouth with the cephalic fins on the sides of its head. The manta ray is **peaceful and harmless**, approaching divers without fear and giving them the privilege of **swimming in its company**.

Sperm Whale

It is 60 feet (18 m) long and eats fish and giant squids. The calves stay with their mothers for more than 10 years.

The sperm whale is a **mammal** that traverses the world's oceans, **migrating seasonally** to follow its prey or to reproduce. It usually prefers waters at least 3,300 feet (1,000 m) deep, where it looks for **giant squids** to hunt. They generally form **groups** made up of females and young males, while **adult males** prefer to live **solitary lives**. Within the group, the **females cooperate** to **nurse** and **protect** the young, which can be **prey to killer whales and great white sharks**.

Marlin

It can reach a maximum length of 16.5 feet (5 m). The long bill, which looks like a sword, is the elongated bone of the upper jaw.

The marlin is an **open-sea sprinter** thanks to its **large tail** and **first dorsal fin**, which slopes sharply down and runs along most of its dark back. It lives in the waters of the Atlantic Ocean, **far from the shore**, where it can chase **shoals of fish** that it stuns with its **long, spear-like bill**. The **females are bigger than the males** and can weigh up to **1,000 pounds (half a ton)**, which is three times heavier than the males. Between May and November, the females lay **millions of eggs**, which have a **diameter of 0.03 inch (1 mm)**.

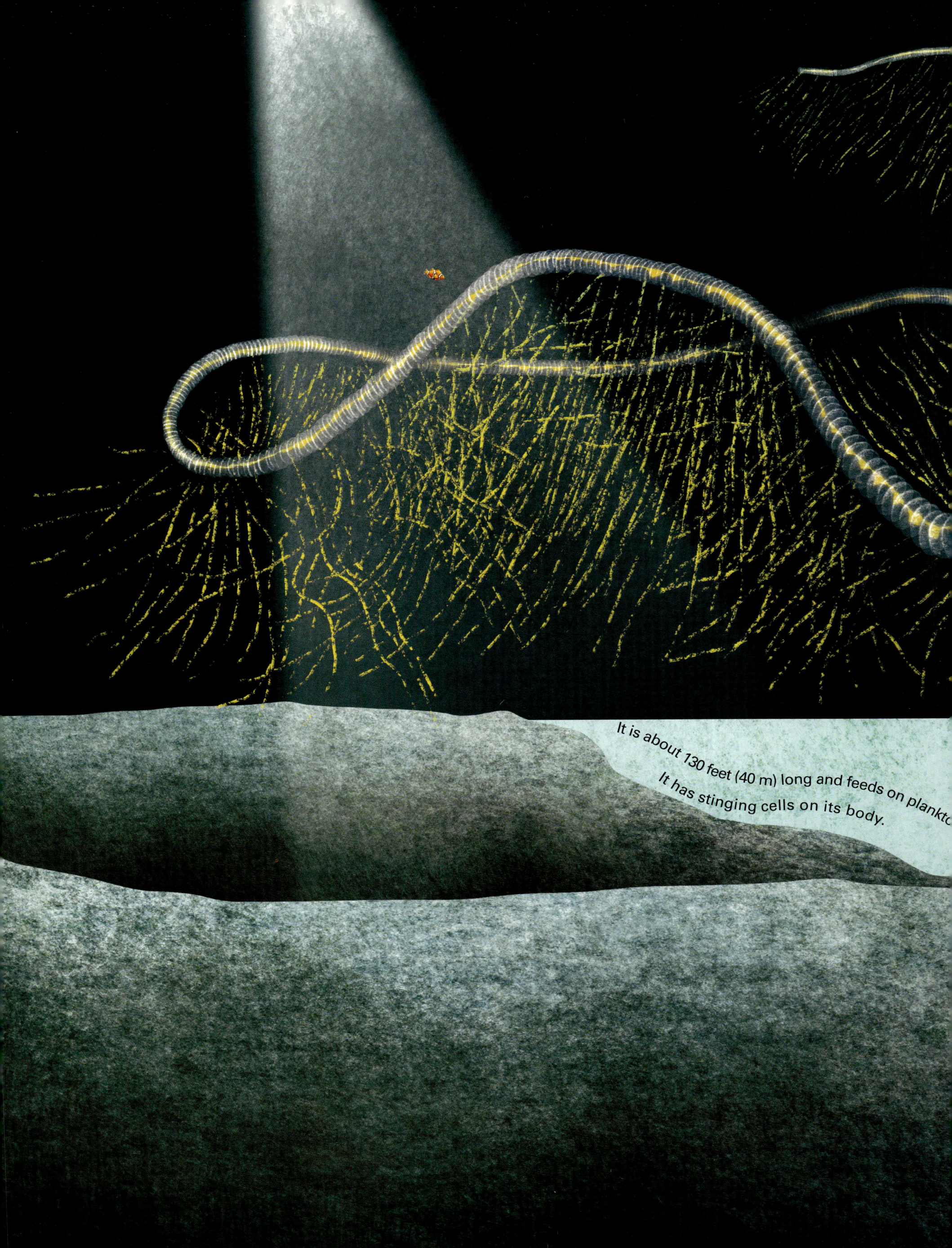

It is about 130 feet (40 m) long and feeds on plankton. It has stinging cells on its body.

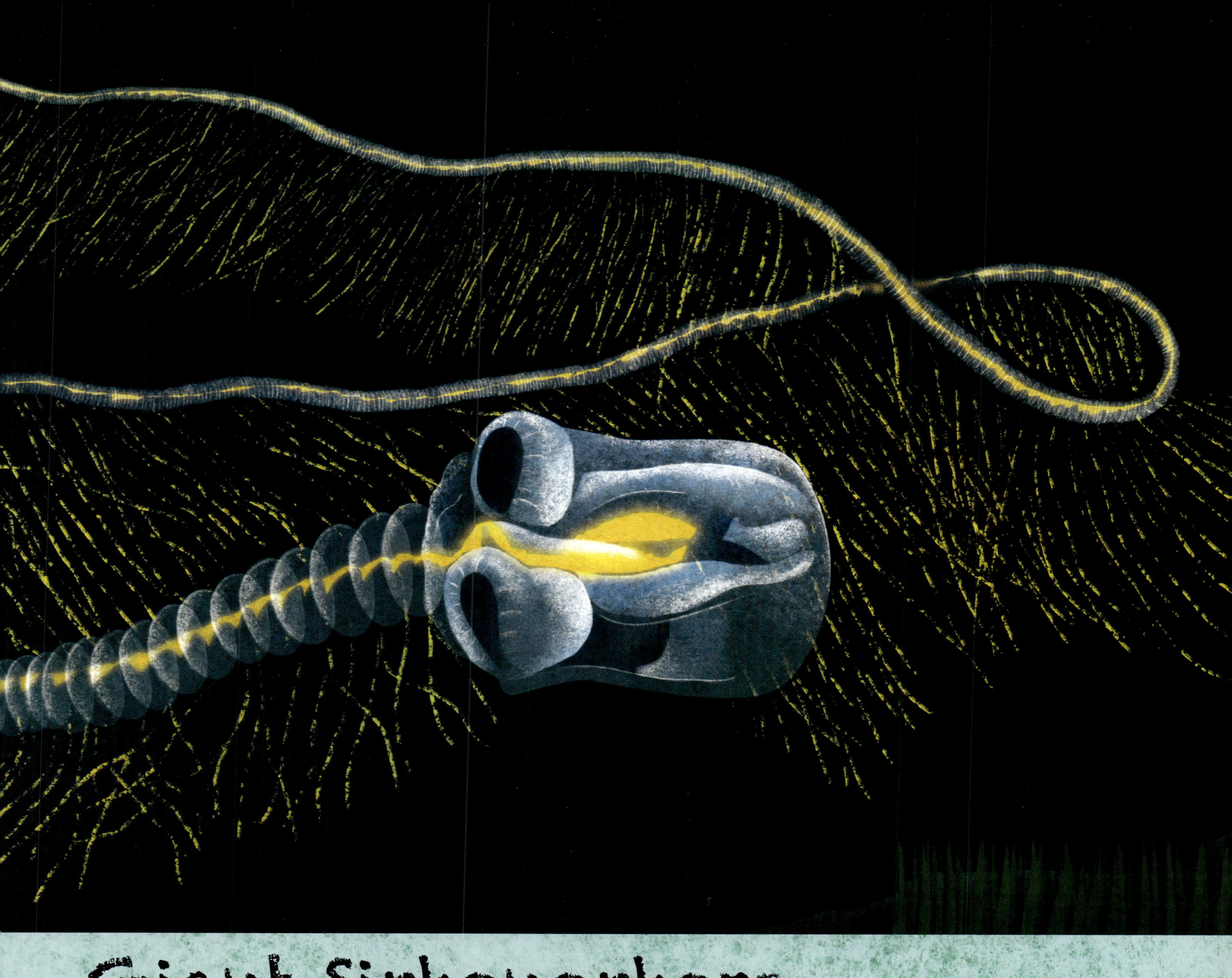

Giant Siphonophore

The giant siphonophore is related to jellyfish and corals and is considered **the longest animal in the world**, even longer than the gigantic blue whale! Its gelatinous body, which looks like a **ribbon** and is as thin as a broomstick, has **numerous** thin and transparent **tentacles** attached to it. It produces **its own light**, and when it bumps into something it emits a **bright blue light** that attracts prey. It is more like a **colony of collaborating individuals** than a single animal, each with its own specialization: some capture food and others digest it; some are responsible for reproduction; and there are even those that decide which direction to move in!

The Australian trumpet is a **gigantic sea snail** with a huge shell—the **largest** and **heaviest in the world**. It lives on the ocean floor off the northern coast of Australia, at depths of up to nearly 100 feet (30 m), and is a predator of large marine worms that live in tubes they build themselves. Adult females produce clusters of large **eggs** that are **the width of a hand** and attach to submerged rocks, shells, or corals. The small larva doesn't hatch directly into the sea. It completes its development **in a capsule** from which the **small snail** comes out, identical to its parents and eventually growing to be the same size as them.

It has a huge shell in which it can reach a length of 35.5 inches (90 cm). It feeds on marine worms.

Australian Trumpet

Giant Oarfish

It can reach a length of 36 feet (11 m) and is the longest bony fish in the world.

Its flesh is almost jelly-like.

The long **crown-like** tendrils on its head and the **bright red dorsal fin** that runs along the length of its body, resembling a **regal cloak**, make this fish the king of herrings, another name for the giant oarfish! With a body so long and flattened it looks like a **ribbon**, it is a very unusual creature that has always ignited the imagination of sailors; it is likely that the various legends about **gigantic sea serpents** derived from the rare sightings of this fish. It is actually a **harmless animal** that lives in very deep waters, swimming with **undulating movements** in search of small prey like krill. It only swims near the surface when ill or dying.

It is 59 feet (18 m) in length. It has the biggest eyes in the animal world, each about the size of a basketball.

Giant Squid

The giant squid is considered the **largest mollusk in the world**. It lives in very deep and cold oceans, at a depth of up to 330 feet (1,000 m). Like all squids, it has a **crown of tentacles** on its head, two of which it uses to feed. These can reach a length of **33 feet (10 m)**, much longer than the other tentacles and even the body itself. The squid launches itself onto its prey and, once caught, pulls it towards the mouth, which has a **strong beak** that can crush anything that comes near it. And if that wasn't enough, it has **lots of tiny teeth** that break down the meal even more before it is swallowed.

It can't move its neck from side to side, so it has to turn its whole body to look behind it. Including the tail, its body can measure 11.5 feet (3.5 m). It eats aquatic plants.

Manatee

The manatee is a **marine mammal** that is also known as the "**sea cow**" due to its chubby body and considerable weight, which can be as much as 1,300 pounds (600 kg). It is **not aggressive** at all and lives in shallow coastal waters, where it spends most of its time **eating** or **resting**. After a 13-month pregnancy, females give birth to **just one calf at a time**, which is cared for by the mother for **two years**. Although it is a **predominantly solitary** animal, the manatee occasionally interacts with its own kind, with which it can communicate through **lively chirps**, **whistles,** and **squeaks**, and even **play**.

Napoleon Fish

You can easily recognize the Napoleon fish due to its **enormous size**; its **large, full lips**; and the protruding **hump on its forehead**, which becomes increasingly prominent as the fish gets older. The color of the **males** can range from **bright green** to opaque green, with shades of blue and violet. The **females** and the **young**, on the other hand, are more often **orangey-red**. They live **in pairs** or in **small groups** of up to seven individuals.

It measures 5 feet (1.5 m) and can weigh as much as 660 pounds (300 kg). It can live for up to 100 years.

Giant Clam

The giant clam is a **bivalve mollusk** whose body is inside a **brightly colored yellow, red, green, blue, pink, and brown** shell. It lives in **symbiosis** with a **certain kind of algae**, providing them with shelter in exchange for the food they produce through **photosynthesis**. However, it also obtains food by itself, filtering microorganisms from the seawater. The giant clam's **shell** is very **robust** and **heavy**, and the valves **open** and **close very slowly**. Giant clams reproduce by releasing **millions of eggs** into the water, of which **only a few** will result in larvae that reach **adulthood**.

It is 10 feet (3 m) long and looks like a snake because it doesn't have pelvic or pectoral fins.

Giant Moray

The giant moray prefers to live in coral reefs in warm, shallow ocean waters. When it is young, the body is **light brown** with large **dark spots**, but as the spots grow, they thicken, creating **a leopard-skin effect**. Despite having a long and heavy body, it is **very flexible** and moves with agility in the water. During the day, the giant moray prefers to rest in its burrow, while it **spends the night hunting**. As it has **poor vision** due to its small eyes, it relies on its **very developed sense of smell** while it lies motionless, waiting to **ambush** its prey.

It can reach a length of 40 feet (12 m). The skin on its back is almost 4 inches (10 cm) thick.

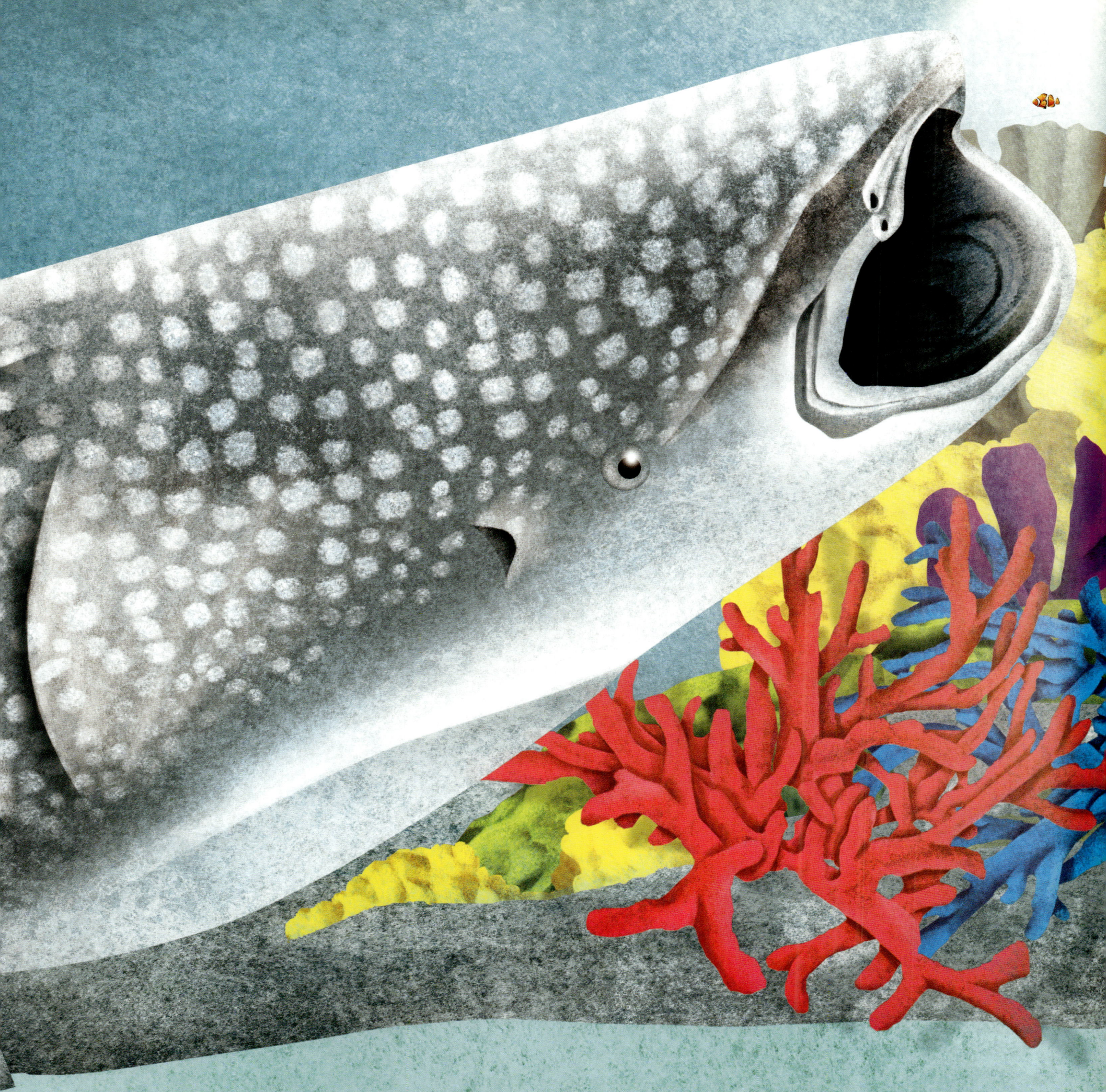

Whale Shark

The whale shark is the largest fish in the world. Despite being a shark, it is docile and patient. It has more than 3,000 teeth, each one about the size of a match head. However, none of these teeth are used for chewing. In fact, despite their enormous size, whale sharks only eat tiny organisms such as plankton, shrimp, and small fish, which they filter from the water with their gills before swallowing and digesting them. They usually swim lazily with their mouths open so they can effortlessly swallow any food that comes into their path.

It can reach a width of 13 feet (4 m).
It is able to grow back lost limbs.

Japanese Spider Crab

The Japanese spider crab is known for being the **largest arthropod in the world**. It has a **pear-shaped** body that is narrower towards the head. The legs are **very long and thin**, and they grow longer as the crab ages. It is a **very peaceful** creature, spending most of its time wandering along the ocean floor in search of food because **it cannot swim**. This large crustacean doesn't usually hunt, preferring to collect dead and decaying organisms from the ocean floor.

This **large cephalopod**'s ideal habitat is ocean floors covered with **soft mud, sand, or gravel**, where there are **also rocks** that the animal can use to make a den. It generally loves to be close to large expanses of algae, up to a depth of 4,900 feet (1,500 m). It is usually a **reddish color**, but it can change its color and the intensity when it feels threatened, so as to frighten the aggressor or to camouflage itself. The eyes are on the **sides** of its large head and provide **extremely sharp vision**. It is a **solitary** and **very shy** animal: it often stays **inside its den** for weeks on end.

Francesca Cosanti

Born in Martina Franca, Italy, in 1985, she attended a multimedia illustration and animation course at the European Institute of Design in Rome, followed by an illustration course at the Academy of Illustration Officina b5 (Rome) and various intensive courses held by internationally renowned illustrators. She has been working as an illustrator since 2005, at the same time teaching in various schools as an expert in illustration and techniques, advertising graphics, and multimedia software. In 2007, she won first prize for her logo for the Department of European Policies at the Presidency of the Italian Council of Ministers. She currently works as an illustrator in publishing and advertising, and in her free time she dedicates herself to her passions: travel, food, swimming, reading, photography, and long walks. In recent years she has illustrated several books for White Star Kids.

VMB Publishers® is a registered trademark property of White Star s.r.l.

© 2020 White Star s.r.l.
Piazzale Luigi Cadorna, 6 - 20123 Milan, Italy
www.whitestar.it

Translation: TxTradurre, Rome
Editing: Michele Suchomel-Casey

All rights reserved. No part of this publication may be reproduced, stored in a retrieval system or transmitted in any form or by any means, electronic, mechanical, photocopying, recording or otherwise, without written permission from the publisher.

ISBN 978-88-540-4425-8
1 2 3 4 5 6   24 23 22 21 20

Printed in Heshan, China

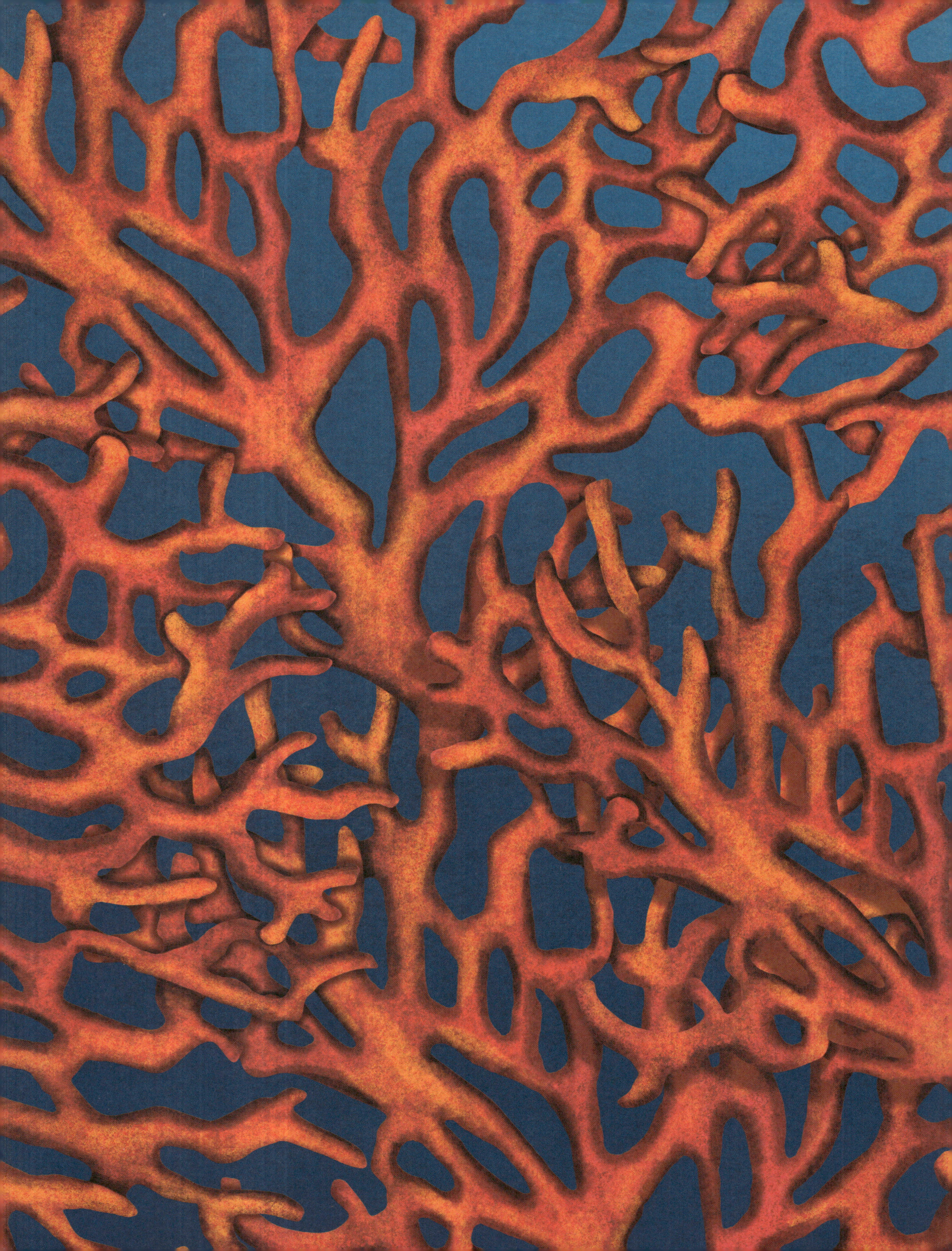